The Life
and Witness
of Saint Maria
Goretti

The Life and Witness of Saint Maria Goretti

Our Little Saint of the Beatitudes

FR. JEFFREY KIRBY, STL

TAN Books
Charlotte, North Carolina

Unless otherwise noted, Scripture quotations are from the Revised Standard Version of the Bible—Second Catholic Edition (Ignatius Edition). Copyright © 2006 Division of Christian Education of the National Council of the Churches of Christ in the United States of America. Used by permission. All rights reserved.

Cover illustration: Original art commissioned by the Shrine of Our Lady of Guadalupe. Painted by Artist: Noah Buchanan. © Shrine of Our Lady of Guadalupe, in La Crosse, Wisconsin.

Cover design by Caroline Kiser

ISBN: 978-1-61890-754-7

Cataloging-in-Publication data on file with the Library of Congress

Printed and bound in the United States of America

TAN Books
Charlotte, North Carolina
www.TANBooks.com
2015

To My Nieces:
Skylar, Kelsey, and Julia

"The wolf shall dwell with the lamb, and the leopard shall lie down with the kid, and the calf and the lion and the fatling together, and a little child shall lead them."
Isaiah 11:6

Contents

Introduction

This book is about Maria Goretti, a small saint with a great witness. In our world that oftentimes struggles with its fallen nature and seeks out sparks of hope or kindness, her Christian witness shines like the morning dawn that breaks through the night's darkness.

St. Maria Goretti offers each of us a testimony of holiness, exemplified by her purity and mercy. It is the testimony of her life lived in Jesus Christ and sealed by her own blood. Quoting the sacred liturgy, it is the testimony of a sacrifice acceptable to God "for the praise and glory of His name and for our good and the good of all His holy Church."

In the Sacred Scriptures, the Prophet Isaiah tells us that peace will come and the wolf will dwell with the lamb, the leopard with the kid, the calf with the lion and the fatling, and "a little child shall lead them" (11:6). The Lord Jesus fulfills this prophecy in His public ministry when He teaches: "Truly, I say to you, unless you become like children, you will never enter the kingdom of heaven" (Mt 18:3).

Maria Goretti is one such child who leads us, who shows us how to be a disciple of Jesus Christ. She died at age twelve. She grew up in a poor farming family and was unable to read or write. Maria Goretti would not otherwise have been known to the world if her outstanding virtue and heroic witness of purity and mercy did not shine out from her small town to the ends of the earth and through the course of the past century and beyond.

St. Maria Goretti is a witness to each of us—of every age and culture, of every economic and social status, of every level of discipleship and desire for holiness—of what it means to be a Christian in our world today. Our little saint is an example and encouragement to each of us who struggle to live a life of virtue, who want to live in purity of heart, who want to forgive or be forgiven; in summary, to all of us who seek the face of God and strive to live fully human lives in Jesus Christ.

A Brief Biography

Throughout her life, Maria Goretti was known for her physical beauty, strong work ethic, deep piety, and cheerfulness that was always tempered by a strong sense of responsibility. Due to these features in her character, she was sometimes affectionately called "the little old lady."

In her family, Maria was the third of seven children. She was born in 1890 to a struggling farming family in the region around Ancona on the eastern side of Italy. Due to the growing poverty of the family, the Gorettis sold their farm and sought to become hired hands on the farmlands of others. This led them to Le Ferriere, near Nettuno, on the western side of Italy. In the marshlands of this region, the family was finally able to find employment.

The work was long and hard, however, and eventually the Gorettis had to welcome Giovanni Serenelli and his son, Alessandro, into their home as partners to share in the farm's labor. Sadly, the extra help made little difference in lightening the workload, and the health of Maria's father worsened. Eventually, he succumbed to the prevalent malaria of the region. Luigi Goretti died when his saintly daughter was only nine years old. Maria's mother, Assunta, and her siblings were at the mercy of Giovanni Serenelli and his son.

Life was very difficult for the Gorettis. Giovanni was an alcoholic and was dismissive and abrupt to Assunta and her children. He demanded that the widow and her older children work in the fields. He instructed that Maria, as the oldest girl, should stay at the house and care for domestic duties and the youngest child. Giovanni's son, Alessandro, who was in his late teens, had a violent temper and was addicted to pornography. Unknown to Assunta, he regularly made inappropriate comments to Maria and twice propositioned her towards lewd acts.

On July 5, 1902, while Giovanni, Assunta, and the older children were out working in the fields, Alessandro returned to the house knowing that Maria would be alone watching the youngest child. Alessandro carried a knife and attempted to rape Maria. She refused and told him that it would be a sin. She was more worried about offending God than about her physical safety. She fought

Alessandro and, in his rage, he brutally stabbed her fourteen times.

Alessandro went and hid while Assunta and Giovanni, responding to Maria's screams, returned to find the young girl alive but covered in her own blood. She was rushed to the local hospital, and the surgeons were shocked that she was still alive. The doctors attempted to save her life and began surgery without anesthesia. Little Maria survived for a day in excruciating pain. She told her mother that she forgave Alessandro, and she died in the peace of Jesus Christ, clutching a crucifix and an image of Mary.

A Witness and a Workbook on Holiness

In these pages we are going to dive into the amazing life of this little saint and her powerful witness. The different chapters will highlight the various aspects of her life and devotion. To help share the story of this virgin martyr, we will use the eight Beatitudes of St. Matthew's Gospel (5:3–12).

The Beatitudes, known as the way of Jesus Christ, will serve as an outline of the saint's narrative. Each of the eight Beatitudes will serve as a guidepost for each of the eight chapters of the book, and will be a focal point from which the inspiring life and witness of St. Maria Goretti will be described and elucidated.

Unlike other biographies, however, our book will not stop at just the narrative of this saint's life. We will go one step further. In each of the chapters of the book, Maria's witness and example will be applied to our own discipleship.

St. Maria Goretti is not a saint to be pitied, but rather one to be emulated. The following chapters will explore the vast areas of our own lives and discipleship where the example, prayers, and encouragement of this little saint can help us grow closer to God and our neighbors. We want to apply and truly live in our own lives the inspiring story and witness of St. Maria Goretti.

Our "American" Saint

St. Maria Goretti is rightly called one of the American saints. Here's a brief explanation. The Battle of Anzio of World War II was an intense and sustained conflict that eventually led to not only an Allied victory, but also the loosening of the grip that the Axis powers had on the Italian peninsula. Occurring in 1944, it would be one of the signature battles that marked the end of the European theater of the war. The battle and the subsequent encampment in Anzio led many American soldiers to visit local towns, including Nettuno, where the shrine of St. Maria Goretti is located.

Many American soldiers, still in the midst of war, turned to the little martyr and asked for her intercession and protection. Many of them sought her help in keeping a purity of heart by avoiding pornography and lewd conduct in the military camps.

The devotion to St. Maria Goretti grew in the United States because of the spiritual communion formed between this little saint and so many of the American soldiers who brought her story and witness back home with them after the war.

To this day, a person could visit the shrine of St. Maria Goretti in Nettuno and, after about a thirty-minute walk, could be at the American foreign cemetery in Anzio. This is the second largest American foreign cemetery in the world (second only to Normandy).

In light of this history, we could spiritually call St. Maria Goretti one of the American saints. What a blessing it is that she will be visiting the United States— her spiritual home—for a Pilgrimage of Mercy in 2015.

A Personal Note

In writing this book, it's important for me to be transparent. I should let the reader know that I'm not writing as a church historian or a biographer. In writing this book, I'm writing the story of a friend, a saintly friend that I have spent a lot of time with and whose prayers and witness have helped me.

As a seminarian at the Pontifical North American College in Rome, I made frequent visits to Nettuno and to the shrine of St. Maria Goretti. Honestly, it was an inexpensive train ticket and a way to leave the hustle and bustle of the Roman metropolis. More importantly, Nettuno and the shrine of the saint was always a place of overwhelming tranquility. I knew it was a place of peace, and I always felt very comfortable there, like being at home. The shrine is right near the water, which is always calming, and the people of Nettuno have a warm and ready hospitality.

St. Maria Goretti's presence is tangible at the shrine. After my visits there, I always left wanting to live a better Christian life.

That's why I've written this book. In sharing the story of this great little saint, I hope every reader will be inspired by the purity, fortitude, and mercy of St. Maria Goretti. I hope her Christian witness will inspire our own discipleship so that, in our own way, we too might put our mark on salvation history.

CHAPTER ONE

The Simplicity of the Goretti Family and the Call to Every Christian Family

"Blessed are the poor in spirit, for
theirs is the kingdom of heaven."
Matthew 5:3

Simplicity of Life

The seduction of comfort and material possessions are strong in the fallen heart of humanity. The tension between "to be" and "to have" is a great battle, one that often ends up with the "having" and controlling of things winning. The goal of such a wayward drive is to build one's own kingdom and to enthrone one's own ego as the sole rule of life.

Such a drive was not found in the material and spiritual poverty of the Goretti family. Luigi and Assunta Goretti, along with Maria and their other children, worked hard for their sustenance and sought to always be a consolation to those in need. Rather than their own egos, the Gorettis sought God's will, and instead of constructing their own kingdom, this holy family desired to receive and spread the kingdom of heaven.

Our work and the things of this world are given as a way for us to encounter Jesus Christ and grow in holiness. They can assist us in maturing in virtue and help us flourish as just human beings. Work and property are intended by God to be a means for the benefit of others, especially for families. In working and owning property, we become stewards of God's Providence, which is His fatherly care of creation. In understanding our own stewardship, our labor and ownership of things should be marked by a keen sense of justice and temperance. These virtues in turn lead us to solidarity with those oppressed by poverty.

In avoiding our stewardship of the things of this world, and the virtues that should accompany it, we feed a dark and excessive appetite for pleasant things that goes beyond reason and propriety. We empower a passion within us for riches and the power that comes with them. Giving expression to this misguided internal drive is the raw amassing of earthly goods without moderation or limit. Such a fallen spiritual state does not allow a person to rejoice at another's good, and it refuses true charity and concern for the vulnerable and one's neighbor.

This was not the life of St. Maria Goretti and her holy family. In their lives, they sought a purification and ordering of their hearts and desires. As a Christian family, they pursued virtue and wanted hearts that were far away from greed and envy. They knew that Jesus Christ could be in the simplicity of life: in honest work, selfless service, and in generosity to the poor. The Gorettis were satisfied with little. They desired only God and His kingdom in their lives.

The Goretti Family

Many things can motivate a person or a family. For the Goretti family it was a strong devotion to Jesus Christ and His Blessed Mother. From this piety, the family sought to live a simple life in God.

Luigi and Assunta married in their hometown of Corinaldo, on the eastern side of Italy. They had a small plot of land, started their life together, and readily welcomed children. The farming was hard work, but they owned the land and they were together. Maria and her siblings helped in the field and with the duties of the house. They were a family. Everyone had a place, and everyone had a responsibility.

This young family had no comforts or extra rations in their lives. Many things that other people considered necessities, they had to regularly live without. The Gorettis, however, never complained or indulged in self-pity, nor resented the blessings of others. Instead, they were filled with gratitude and every evening prayed the Rosary together as a family in praise and thanksgiving to God for what they did have and for His blessings in their lives. The Goretti family lived in true simplicity of life. They sought the kingdom of God and not its caricature in excessive riches or empty ownership of the things of this world.

When Maria was six years old, however, the family could not make ends meet and made the heart wrenching decision to sell their land and seek employment in the fields of someone else. Luigi searched and eventually found a job opportunity in Le Ferriere on the western coast of Italy. With heavy hearts, the Gorettis had to move. They left the land of their families and their birth, of all that they knew and loved, and went to an unknown place filled with people who did not seem to care about them. It was a departure that deepened their own sense of simplicity of life and of holding God's kingdom as their only possession.

After arriving in Le Ferriere, the family saw that the fields were in marshlands. In order for them to survive and live off of the profits from the farming, there would need to be very little spending and a lot of hard work. The family lived in an old cheese factory and labored to spend as little as possible and to make every resource as beneficial as possible. In its poverty and in all its difficulties, the Goretti family saw God's Providence and thanked Him. They sought to find His goodness and grace in their many needs and they joyfully lived as inheritors of a greater kingdom.

Workshop for Holiness

The simplicity of life shown by the Goretti family is a model and a call to every Christian family. In its desire to live the Beatitude "Blessed are the poor in spirit, for theirs is the kingdom of heaven," the Christian family is called to look at its own heart and to question how the battle between "to be" and "to have" is being waged in its life. While a family may not be called to the radical material poverty of the Gorettis, each Christian family is summoned to a simplicity of life. In our families, have excess and comfort replaced temperance and justice?

The Goretti family saw everything as a blessing from God, and they labored, even amidst incredible hardship, to see God's Providence and to seek His kingdom above all else. This is the foundational and life-giving principle that should inspire, guide, and enliven the Christian family in our world today. How are we doing?

As a help to our own efforts for simplicity in the Christian home, this chapter will conclude with this Examination of Conscience:

EXAMINATION OF CONSCIENCE

- Do I see God as the one who has given me the blessings of my life? Or do I only credit my blessings as the results of my hard work or ingenuity?

- What do I most treasure in this life? Does my way of life (work ethic, spending, and saving) reflect these priorities?

- What do I principally spend my money on? Do I allow myself to be guided by justice and temperance in my spending and saving?

- How do I react to the possessions of others?

- Do I own things that I never use?

- What responsibilities do I have towards others? Am I attentive to the poor and those in need?

- Is what I own right now enough for me? Too much?

- Do I find myself always wanting what I don't have?

- Am I grateful for the blessings in my life?

- Do I balance my work and income with my spiritual, familial, and social responsibilities?

- Do I have a consumer mentality, where everything is marked by give-and-take? Am I generous to others without expectations of repayment?

- Do I honor the contracts and promises I have made to others?

- Do I fulfill my work responsibilities with honesty and excellence?

- Have I made good on my debts?

- Do I use credit out of vanity and a desire for acceptance?

CHAPTER TWO

The Loss of Luigi Goretti and the Vocation of the Christian Father

"Blessed are those who mourn,
for they shall be comforted."
Matthew 5:4

Christian Fatherhood

The death of a loved one leaves a scar on the human heart. The loss of a parent is especially trying. Such a loss leads to a re-definition of what life will be for us without the very one who gave us life in the first place.

This was the experience and story of Maria Goretti and her family when her father died from malaria. Maria acutely felt his loss and sought to console her mother and siblings.

In our contemporary culture, fatherhood is unknown to many and neglected or even outright dismissed by others. Absent or disinterested fathers hurt their families and confuse their children.

The role of the Christian father is a vocation given by God. In his Letter to the Ephesians, St. Paul teaches us: "For this reason I bow my knees before the Father, from whom every family in heaven and on earth is named" (3:14–15). As every family is named by God, so the father of a family is given a position of responsibility and service.

The Christian father is also a Christian husband, and his first service is to his wife, who is his equal in dignity. The man is called to love his wife "as Christ loved the Church," which means he must be willing to lay down his life for her and their children (cf. Eph 5:25). The husband is called to show deference and deep affection towards his wife and the mother of his children. In showing such loving kindness to his wife, the husband models the tranquility that should be the mark of the Christian home. From the man's marital vocation, flows his service as a Christian father.

As the father of the Christian family, which is a domestic church, a man is further commissioned by God to show faithful care and attention to his children. He is to be an exemplar of prayer and virtue. As the royal priest of a domestic church, along with his wife, the Christian father is to lead his family to God by regular participation at Mass, frequent Confession, family prayer, and heroic virtue. The man is given the grace to be a prudent servant of God, guiding and guarding the spiritual life of his wife and children.

As a Christian father, the man is called by God to work and provide for his family. He has the privilege in

Jesus Christ to allow his work to be a daily expression of his love as he supports his wife and family.

In all the responsibilities and duties within his vocation as a Christian father, the man is called to show a gentle strength to his wife and children, and assure harmony within the family as well as peace in the home. In his paternal witness, a father's children should always know and be able to rely on his deep love, acceptance, generosity of time and affection, patience, mercy, and willing support. In the Christian father, despite his own sinfulness and weakness, children should always see a reflection of God himself.

The blessing the Church offers to fathers on the baptism of their children summarizes his vocation well:

> God is the giver of all life, human and divine. May He bless the father of this child. He and his wife will be the first teachers of their child in the ways of faith. May they be also the best of teachers, bearing witness to the faith by what they say and do, in Christ Jesus our Lord. Amen.

The Goretti Family

Luigi and Assunta Goretti were from the little district of Corinaldo, in the region known as "The Marshes" on the eastern side of the Italian peninsula. Due in part by the close proximity of the Holy House of Loreto, which is the house attested to have been the home of Jesus, Mary, and Joseph when they lived in Nazareth, the area has always been strong in its devotion to Mary and the Holy Family.

Luigi understood his vocation as a husband and father. He knew very clearly his responsibility to care for his wife. He welcomed children and showed them a father's love. Luigi worked hard in the fields and returned home exhausted, but he always made time to greet his wife and children. Although fatigued from his farm labor, after having his evening meal, he gave special attention to each of his children and would always pray a Rosary with them before going to bed. Before sleeping, Luigi and Assunta would also pray together for their children. Luigi sought to always rely on God and worked tirelessly to be an instrument of God's love and mercy to his family.

When the work and property in Corinaldo could no longer support the family, Luigi understood his Christian duties and looked for employment. He eventually found work on the farms of a nobleman and took his family to the eastern coast of Italy. When the family arrived and saw that the farm was in the marshlands, Luigi immediately set about his work. He labored tirelessly in order to properly prepare the fields for farming. The young husband and father worked himself to illness and had to suspend his work so that he could recuperate. The landowner then demanded that Luigi take on extra help, so Giovanni and Alessandro Serenelli moved into the Goretti home and began to work with Luigi as business partners.

It was not an ideal arrangement. The Serenellis did not have the piety and virtue of the Gorettis. Luigi created boundaries between the two families so that his children would not be influenced by bad examples. He sought to make the arrangement work since he needed the profit from the harvest to provide food for his family. Luigi's kindness and respect, however, were not reciprocated.

Sadly, malaria eventually overtook Luigi. In his last few days, he was filled with anguish for his family. He was leaving them without financial stability, with questionable business partners, and away from their extended family. Luigi received the Last Rites and before he died he told his wife, "Go back to Corinaldo." Unfortunately, the young widow did not have the resources to return to her hometown, and the bereaved family was left under the yoke of Giovanni Serenelli and his son.

All of the children in the Goretti family took Luigi's death very hard, but none took it as deeply as Maria. She revered her father and loved him as only an eldest daughter could. Maria was always a tenderhearted person, and while her father was sick, she would run the several miles to Nettuno to get him medicine. During his illness, Maria would forget to eat or sleep as she served him and the family. Maria was only nine when Luigi Goretti died, but she entered a new phase of her own life. While she missed her father immensely, she became more determined in her charity towards her mother and siblings. With her father gone, Maria knew that his paternal responsibilities would need to be carried by others, and she was very willing to serve and protect her family.

Even as the family suffered under the Serenelli men and the workload intensified, Maria never forgot her father. Whenever she went into town to sell eggs, she would stop at the cemetery where he was buried and pray for him. The Goretti family still prayed a Rosary together every night, and each night Maria would pray a second whole Rosary alone just for her father.

The witness of this Christian father continued on through the life and martyrdom of his beloved daughter. The life Luigi modeled made a lasting impression on his children, and Maria would remember this witness even to the moment of her death. She would stand fast against sin even when confronted with the point of a knife and death. She would not abandon Jesus Christ and her purity of faith and morals. The story of her father, his hard work and virtue, his prayer and kindness, gave the little saint the strength and power to fight evil and to bear her own perpetual witness to goodness.

After the brutal attack against Maria and her purity, as she lay dying in the hospital, she turned spiritually to her father. Luigi's legacy of faith and virtue lived on, and spoken in great affection, one of Maria's last words was "Daddy!" Perhaps, in the communion of saints, her father was there with her, to welcome his beloved daughter turned virgin-martyr into heaven.

Workshop for Holiness

We live in a time when the Christian family is both under siege from outside and under attack from within. The family must both discern negative and dark influences, as well as its own commitment to Jesus Christ. We live in a world where falsehood is described as enlightenment, parental neglect is praised as trust, and moral permissiveness is veiled as freedom. In such an arena, Christian parents are torn between their faith and the protection on their children's virtue on one hand, and the aggressive currents of our secular society and its pressure on the other. In this tension, Christian parents must rely on the rule of faith and seek what good things will praise God. They should be cautious about the vanity, human respect, and fallen praise of this world. The Christian parent is always called to give witness to Jesus Christ and to both guard and guide the spiritual and moral development of their children.

In particular, the Christian father should feel the weight of his responsibility and seek to imitate the holy men of our faith, such as Luigi Goretti.

As a help to Christian parents in their vocation, this chapter concludes with this Examination of Conscience:

EXAMINATION OF CONSCIENCE

- Do I realize and accept that my marriage and parenthood are vocations from God?

- Do I show deference and respect to my spouse?

- Do I see my spouse as my equal and seek harmony in my marriage?

- Do I take seriously my responsibilities to guide and guard the spiritual and moral development of my children?

- Am I negatively influenced in my Christian duties by the opinions and comments of other parents or people in my society?

- Do I take my children to Sunday Mass and ensure that they regularly go to Confession? Have I allowed sports or other forms of recreation to supplant or distract from the spiritual duties to my children and family?

- Have I taught my children how to pray?

- Do I communicate with my children and know what people or sources are influencing them?

- Have I been attentive to whom my children are friends with and with whom they are dating?

- Have I given clear boundaries to my children on what is morally right and/ or age-appropriate signs of affection for others?

- Have I given my children a positive example of the value of work?

- Do I cause needless tension or fights in my marriage or family?

- Do I supervise how my children use the internet and television? Have I taught them to use Christian moral truth as a norm for their entertainment and communication with others?

- Have I modeled and taught my children how to show kindness and mercy to others?

- Have I interfered in the freedom of my children to pursue a priestly or religious vocation?

CHAPTER THREE

The Meekness of Hard Work and the Christian Work Ethic in Our Day

"Blessed are the meek, for they shall inherit the earth."
Matthew 5:5

The Christian Understanding of Work

The Christian faith has always seen work as a duty and privilege given by God. It helps us to honor Him for the gifts and talents that we have generously received from Him. Every human person is called to work in some shape or form. Work distinguishes us from all other creatures since it flows from our dignity as sons and daughters of God made in His image. Work prolongs the continual work of creation by subduing the earth both with and for one another.

Human work can also be redemptive. It has been made a path of holiness by Jesus Christ who labored as a carpenter. We live and show ourselves as disciples of the Lord Jesus by carrying our cross daily in the work we are called to fulfill. In working out our salvation "with fear and trembling," we accept the hardships of our work and allow grace to transform us (cf. Phil 2:12).

Work is for the flourishing of the human person and society, and so the person does not solely exist to work, as if he were just a machine. Work calls us to community life and to solidarity with our neighbors. In working with others, we exchange human goods and virtue with one another. We help to build a civil society, a true civilization of love. In these efforts, we extend our Christian witness beyond our families and seek to cooperate in human development, as well as to share the truths of faith with all people. And so, our work can be a means of grace not only for ourselves but also for others as we offer these labors to Jesus Christ for our loved ones and for those in need.

From our work, every human person should be able to receive his "daily bread," meaning that from our work, we should be able to provide support to ourselves and our families. This is a principle of justice inherent in the nature of work itself. It is the temporal purpose of work and the hope of every worker.

The Goretti Family

The Goretti family understood the value and spiritual power of work. Luigi and Assunta worked as a team between the fields and the housework. Maria and her siblings were also taught the importance of good work and the Christian virtues born from it.

When Maria was six and the family moved to Le Ferriere, they saw the flat and empty panorama of the

Pontine Marshes. The land seemed lifeless. It was low-lying and swampy. The heat was intense. There were no trees, which meant no shade. Luigi and his family realized very quickly that they were not in Corinaldo anymore and they would not be working on their own little plot of land. They were hired workers and would now farm on someone else's fields; fields that, to their misfortune, were not favorable to farming.

Before the Gorettis arrived, the land had not been cared for in over three years. The ditches had been neglected to such a degree that they no longer carried off the excess water. Luigi started his work on the ditches since they were needed for the fields. He exerted great effort to bring the farmland under control. After the ditch digging, however, there was more work to be done.

With the ditches in order, Luigi began to plow. He plowed several acres of land and began to sow wheat and barley. Once the sowing was done, however, there was still even more work to be done.

With the fields in some semblance of order, Luigi began to work on the buildings that were in severe disrepair. He replaced roofs, fixed the lofts, and renovated the stables. Luigi was a good man who worked hard to care for his family.

Sadly, Luigi's work wore him down and he began to have a cough and fever. Frustrated with himself, he was unable to work and was confined to bed. On account of this recovery time, Luigi couldn't fully harvest the fields, and when the nobleman came to inspect the land, he was angered by Luigi's apparent neglect of the fields. The nobleman demanded that Luigi accept help and sent him the father and son Serenelli. Luigi purposely worked on his tasks alone so that the profit from the harvest would help his family and provide them with some security. Now, he had to succumb, not only to the beginning of malaria, but to these dark and suspicious business partners and housemates.

Luigi labored hard to find the energy to begin work again and sought to be fair and kind to the Serenellis. He was a strong worker who knew the spiritual and earthly blessings of virtuous work. Luigi worked as a Christian who saw his work as a part of his discipleship and service to the Lord Jesus. He did not indulge in self-pity, envy, or despair. He did not complain over the difficulties in his work. He wanted to give a strong Christian witness to his children, who also worked on the farm as their age would allow, so that they might know the value of good work as a path to holiness.

Workshop for Holiness

In our culture today, it seems that many people want things for which they are not willing to work. The elementary lessons of hard work and consistent effort, of virtue and self-determination, seem to be eclipsed by a societal sloth that expects many things but is willing to give very little.

The virtues that are given by good work done well are a path not only to civility but also to holiness in the Christian life. In work, we find our place in the continued creation of the world, as well as the path of humility and obedience to tasks and to others in authority.

The Goretti family is an exemplar for us of what good work looks like and how it both nurtures and is sustained by Christian discipleship and a life of faith. To help us imitate the good workers of our faith, this chapter concludes with this Examination of Conscience:

EXAMINATION OF CONSCIENCE

- Do I understand my work as a part of my Christian discipleship?

- Do I see my work as a means to provide for my family and fulfill the duties of my state in life?

- Do I model a good Christian work ethic to my spouse and children?

- Do I waste time at work or at home? Do I overwork?

- Have I sought to be a Christian witness to my colleagues and co-workers?

- Have I allowed material possessions to be the purpose of my life?

- Have I indulged in envy, self-pity, or despair over my work or its hardships?

- Do I show respect to my employer/employees?

- Do I give a just wage and proper benefits to my employees?

- Have I squandered my money on wasteful pursuits, gambling, or overspending?

- Have I allowed myself to live beyond my means and the income of my employment?

- Have I been generous to others who are in need?

- Have I misused property or natural resources?

- Have I made restitution on any stealing, cheating, or fraud?

- Have I been responsible with debt and credit?

CHAPTER FOUR

Desiring Holiness in What We Think, Say, and Do

"Blessed are those who hunger and thirst for righteousness, for they shall be satisfied."
Matthew 5:6

Thirsting for Holiness

Holiness is a tangible, practical reality in life. One can see, hear, taste, smell, and encounter holiness. It is more real than any material object, such as a book, chair, or table, since it involves the grace of God that always becomes active and visible in the lives of those who thirst and hunger for God.

Holiness is the meeting point—a radical cooperation—between our freedom and God's grace. Holiness is when God offers each of us an invitation to follow Him and we accept it. When we make the decision to follow Jesus Christ, fanning into flame the graces God has given us, we are called to die to sin, be healed from the wounds it has caused within us, and to live the way of life shown to us by Jesus Christ.

For us to die to sin and follow Jesus Christ, we have to daily take up our cross and live His Paschal Mystery. The Paschal Mystery is the Passion, Death, and Resurrection of Jesus Christ. In our lives, we have to be willing to endure "the passion and death" to our own sin and the areas of darkness within us. If one person struggles with purity and another with mercy, the way we follow the Lord Jesus is by suffering through the passion of lust and callousness so that we die to these bad spirits. In this way, we can live as sons or daughters of the Resurrection. We can walk the path of holiness.

Holiness is marked by love. It is a love of both God and neighbor, a love that is sacrificial and willing to suffer for a greater good. Living a life of love means that we truly love God for His own sake and not because of the consolations or blessings we desire from Him. We love our neighbors, not in disguised egotism, but in selfless service. We love them for the love of God and within our discipleship to the Lord Jesus.

Holiness is also about time and continual conversion. The thirst and hunger for righteousness that begins within us is initiated by God and nurtured by His grace. It is not a competition, we do not determine the timeline, and the results of our cooperation with His grace are all a free gift given by God when and how He chooses. Holiness is following, not leading or pretending to follow, but truly following God in love and surrender.

The Goretti Family

In the Sermon on the Mount, the Lord Jesus describes two options: the wide gate that leads to destruction or the narrow gate that leads to life (see Mt 7:13–14). In his writings, St. Paul develops these two options and describes them as the way of the Spirit that leads to freedom, or the way of the flesh that leads to slavery (see Rom 8:1–17). Later in salvation history, Pope St. John Paul II developed these same two options and named them the culture of life and the culture of death.

These teachings show us that in life we have to decide which path we will follow. With two ways before us, it might be helpful to illustrate each one by using examples. So, we can look at the relationship between mother and daughter, Assunta and Maria; and, between father and son, Giovanni and Alessandro.

Maria and Assunta chose the narrow gate, the way of the Spirit, and the culture of life. While Giovanni and Alessandro chose the wide gate, the way of the flesh, and the culture of death. Let's explore what these ways of life look like in the world.

After Luigi died, Assunta had to work in the fields and Maria took over the household duties. They loved and respected one another. The exchange between Alessandro and Giovanni, however, was marked by mutual animosity and fighting.

Assunta and Maria made the effort to collect the whole family and attend Sunday Mass and to pray a Rosary together every evening as a family. Giovanni and Alessandro never attended worship services and indulged their vanity and pride.

Every evening when Assunta returned from the fields, Maria made sure her siblings ran out and greeted her. She would have dinner prepared and on the table waiting for her mother who was tired from the day's work. Giovanni and Alessandro would return from the fields and isolate themselves, Giovanni drinking and abusing alcohol, while Alessandro entered the addictive world of lust and pornography.

Maria always served her mother and siblings first at the table. She and Assunta would outdo one another in acts of charity. Giovanni and Alessandro served only themselves and were even unjust in the distribution of the profit from the farm.

In the home, Maria was always quick to serve and to do swiftly whatever Assunta asked of her. Her obedience and charity was immediate and generous. Alessandro, however, was aggressive towards his father and the two were in a constant quarrel.

Whenever Maria received gifts from neighbors, such as fruit or eggs, she would always save and share them with Assunta and her siblings. Alessandro and Giovanni, however, were greedy and hoarders. They shared nothing that they received, including a just compensation to Assunta for her work.

Maria was always the last one to go to bed at night. She made sure that her mother had a good night's sleep and that her siblings were all tucked in. Maria sacrificially cared for her family. Alessandro and Giovanni demanded service and were unkind and even tyrannical in their expectations. There was no understanding of service or gentleness about them.

Finally, how did the two groups view each other? Assunta and Maria approached the father and son with caution, but also with peace and compassion. They had forgiving hearts. Giovanni and Alessandro approached the mother and daughter with disdain. They were rude and harsh. The only thing in their hearts were calculations on how much more they could get from this vulnerable mother and her children.

The path to holiness is clear and tangible. While not easy or comfortable, it is worth having a hunger and thirst for this narrow gate. The way of the Spirit always involves a cross, a passion and death, but it merits every sacrifice because there is a resurrection. The culture of life is the culture of holiness. This was the life of our little saint and her gracious mother. We are called to this same holiness.

Workshop for Holiness

Holiness has not received good press in recent years. Oftentimes, holy people are presented as dark and lifeless figures. Holy people are described as those who couldn't make it in life, or who denied themselves everything and were without smiles or joys. This is not holiness. In fact, if we really want to see what living a fully human life looks like, we should look to the saints. They had fun, laughed, had tremendous joys (oftentimes in the midst of sorrows), and they came from every vocation, profession, culture, and spirituality. The saints, our holy ones, are awesome!

The call the Lord Jesus offers to each of us is the invitation to an exciting adventure. We have to decide whether we will fan into flame the graces He's given us, or whether we will decline the invitation and walk away. For those of us who say "yes" and who really hunger and thirst for holiness, the Lord Jesus will bring to completion the good work He has begun in us. We just have to accept the invitation, and then buckle our seatbelts because we're in for a great ride.

And as we follow the path of holiness, the Lord Jesus provides and blesses us with several means by which we can be with Him and receive His grace. The principal gifts given by the Lord Jesus are the seven sacraments: Baptism, Confirmation, Holy Communion, Penance, Holy Matrimony, Holy Orders, and Anointing of the Sick. Other gifts which the Lord Jesus has given us and which we can exercise include regular prayer, reading of the Sacred Scriptures, the exercise of virtue, and selfless service to others.

Each of these are a help to us. As we hunger and thirst for holiness, our chapter concludes with this Examination of Conscience:

EXAMINATION OF CONSCIENCE

- Do I love God with all my heart? Do I truly hunger and thirst for holiness?

- Have I looked for ways in which I can tell others about God?

- Do I let something or someone influence my decisions more than God?

- Do I have false gods in my life that I place before God (i.e., money, power, fame, work, recreation, pleasure, etc.)?

- Do I frequent the sacraments, especially Sunday Mass and regular Confession?

- Do I honor Sunday as a day of rest and family?

- Do I spend time with God in prayer every day?

- Do I take God's name carelessly or uselessly?

- Have I been dismissive or negligent in my education in the Faith? Have I been attentive to the religious instruction of my spouse and children?

- Have I sought to recognize and die to the sins in my life so that I might live as a better Christian?

- Do I look for ways in which I can serve the members of my family and other people in my life?

- Have I looked for ways in which my home can be a domestic church? Have I nurtured a desire for holiness in my spouse and children?

- Do I look for ways to show humility and obedience in my life?

- Do I apologize when I overreact or when I am abrupt or rude to other people?

- Have I been disrespectful or irreverent towards the Church or things pertaining to the Church?

CHAPTER FIVE

The Mercy of Our Little Martyr and her Mother and the Struggle to Forgive Others

"Blessed are those who hunger and thirst for righteousness, for they shall be satisfied."
Matthew 5:6

The Gift of Mercy

As human beings, we are most like God when we show mercy. In our discipleship, we are closest to the Heart of Christ when we forgive others. Our little saint and her godly mother show us the face of mercy.

Mercy is the core of who we are as Christian believers, but what is mercy? Doesn't it suspend justice and legitimize the offense that we or a loved one have suffered? Why are we called to show mercy?

Before we address any specific questions, we should turn to the Lord Jesus Himself. He is "the Way, the Truth, and the Life," and so we desire to learn from him, receive His grace, and follow Him in all the areas of our life, including mercy and forgiveness (cf. Jn 14:6).

In the Sermon on the Mount, the Lord Jesus teaches us: "For with the judgment you pronounce you will be judged, and the measure you give will be the measure you get" (Mt 7:2). This is a challenging summons, and one that is repeated in the Lord's Prayer: "And forgive us our debts, as we also have forgiven our debtors" (Mt 6:12). As Christians we should be so filled with gratitude for the mercy shown to us by God that we are willing to suffer the necessary passion and die to ourselves so that we can sincerely forgive others. The Lord Jesus is our strength and our shepherd. On the Cross, He personified mercy and showed us its beauty and power. In the intensity of His sorrows and sufferings, He cried out: "Father, forgive them; for they know not what they do" (Lk 23:34).

In light of our faith, we have to look at mercy with different eyes. Mercy does not undermine or dismiss justice but rather fulfills it. Justice is the virtue by which we receive what is due to us within the internal rationale and order of loving kindness. The recipient of justice, the one who has been offended, determines the nature and reception of what is due to him. Mercy is allowing justice—what is due to me—to be fulfilled within a broader application of loving kindness. In this way, mercy fulfills justice and allows for the common good to be built up by loving kindness rather than retaliation or violence.

In its very dynamics, mercy gives freedom to both the one who has been offended and the offender. It does not legitimize the offense that has been suffered but provides an arena of healing to the one who was offended, and of conversion and reform to the one who offended.

The Goretti Family

Now, we approach a narrative of great mercy. The story involves a virgin martyr, her murderer, and her loving mother. It is a story that is as shocking in its brutality as it is tender and compelling in its sweetness.

In Le Ferriere, Maria and her family shared the house with Giovanni Serenelli and his son, Alessandro. Alessandro allowed his mind and heart to be warped by lust and violence. On July 5, 1902, he propositioned little Maria and threatened her with a knife. When she refused, Alessandro stabbed her fourteen times. It was a brutal attack, and Maria suffered from her wounds with little pain medication even after being rushed to the hospital.

In the last few hours of her life, when the priest came to administer Last Rites, he asked her: "And you, Maria, do you pardon, from the bottom of your heart, your murderer?" And, in a moment of tremendous grace, little Maria, dying and in great pain, said to the priest: "Yes, I, for the love of Jesus, pardon him. And I desire that he may come with me to heaven," and then continued, "Pardon him, my God, because I have already forgiven him."

Alessandro was taken immediately to jail. He denied that he was involved in the attack on Maria and then claimed to be out of his mind. His attempts to avoid accountability, however, were without success. After a trial, in which he was both foul and offensive in his demeanor, he was sentenced to thirty years in prison. In the first few years of prison, he had a hard heart. He showed no remorse for his sins against Maria Goretti and was monstrous in his behavior.

Alessandro's cynicism enslaved him. He was under a dark cloud of despair and guilt, but mercy would prevail. The very one whose life he took would come to him and help him save his own.

One evening in a dream, Maria came to Alessandro dressed in white, bareheaded, and beaming with great joy. She was walking in a field of lilies and handed several of the lilies to Alessandro. Hesitantly, he received them and, as he did so, the lilies quickly became tongues of fire. He was confused and looked at Maria. She simply smiled and he woke up. Once awake, Alessandro knew exactly what the dream meant. He understood that the lilies were symbols of innocence that were now being offered to him again, while the tongues of fire were symbols of mercy and the purgation he would need to undergo in order to be restored to a life of grace. That very night Alessandro turned to Jesus Christ and begged for mercy. We can imagine St. Maria Goretti rejoicing with the heavenly host over the repentance of this one sinner.

Alessandro lived a good Christian life after his conversion. He served twenty-seven years in prison and was known for his gentleness and kindness to his fellow prisoners. He saw his prison sentence as a way to make reparation for his sin.

After his release from prison, Alessandro went to see Assunta to ask her for mercy in person. Assunta was sitting down to eat when Alessandro knocked on the door. When she opened it, she saw her daughter's murderer on his knees, hands outstretched, sobbing and begging her for mercy. Only God knows what goes through the heart of a mother in such a moment.

Decades earlier, when Maria was with Assunta and they would walk to the local town or cross a field, Assunta was afraid of the snakes. Maria was not afraid and would tell her mother, "Come, Mamma, I will go ahead of you. Just follow me." No doubt, her daughter's witness and this counsel floated in Assunta's heart as she saw Alessandro in front of her. Now, she would once again follow her daughter.

And so Assunta, wanting to be an instrument of mercy like her saintly daughter, helped Alessandro up, brought him into her home, and sat him down to eat the very food she had prepared for herself. When he asked her for mercy, Assunta told Alessandro, "I forgive you because Maria already has."

The next Sunday at Mass, to the shock and renewal of the local community, Assunta joined Alessandro at the Communion rail and both received Holy Communion together. How appropriate that this mercy should be brought to the Altar of God and celebrated within the Eucharistic Banquet, which is the supreme act of mercy and reconciliation. This total expression of mercy from God and from Assunta freed Alessandro from any remaining anguish in his soul. He surrendered his life to

God and joined in the work of the Capuchin friars until his death.

Alessandro lived to be eighty-seven years old, never forgetting the mercy shown to him my Maria and Assunta, and continually relying on the mercy poured upon him by the Lord Jesus Christ.

Workshop for Holiness

In our world today there seems to be a real absence of mercy. Everyone seems intent on a raw sense of justice. People are more concerned with "an eye for an eye, and a tooth for a tooth" than a true conversion of hearts and reconciliation between neighbors. In such a culture, St. Maria Goretti is a sign of contradiction. This little saint stands as a witness and model of what mercy is for the person of good will and especially for the Christian believer.

In our own struggle to accept, find, or to give mercy, we are called to turn to the Lord Jesus. It is only in being bathed in His ocean of mercy that we can have true hearts disposed towards the reception and giving of mercy.

In our own quest to live as instruments of mercy, this chapter concludes with an Examination of Conscience:

EXAMINATION OF CONSCIENCE

- Do I rely on God's grace to be a person of mercy?

- Have I hardened my heart and refused to receive or to give mercy?

- Do I regularly go to Confession to receive God's mercy?

- Do I pray and ask for God's help in moments when I need to give or receive mercy?

- Do I fail to recognize my own weaknesses and see myself as superior to others?

- Do I ask for forgiveness when I have been offensive or hurtful to others?

- Do I recognize the weaknesses of others and try to show them compassion and gentleness?

- Do I hold on to bitterness over past offenses?

- Am I resentful to others, not speaking or making hurtful or offensive comments?

- Do I gossip about offenses or slander the reputation of others?

- Am I accusatory and aggressive to others in their shortcomings or weaknesses?

- Am I inclined to rash judgment of people or situations?

- Do I assume bad intentions or motives in the actions of others?

- Do I pray for my enemies and for those who have hurt me or a loved one?

- Do I give people a new beginning?

CHAPTER SIX

The Blood of Our Martyr and the Battle for Purity in Our Hearts

"Blessed are the pure in heart, for they shall see God."
Matthew 5:8

Purity of Heart

God made our hearts for freedom and for the virtues that flow from it. For us to have a pure heart and to live a fully human life, we have to avoid the attraction and slavery of sin. Of all the inclinations of our fallen nature, none is so seductive or addictive as lust. Simply defined, lust is a desire for sexual pleasure that is sought only for itself and not as a true expression of love for another.

Our virgin-martyr stands in contradiction to this wayward desire so often indulged by darkened hearts. By her heroic life, Maria shows us "the more excellent way" of love expressed in chastity and purity of heart (see 1 Cor 12:31).

Our sexual powers affect all the aspects of our bodies and souls. They are powers given to us so that we can express a self-donation of affection and communion within the sacrament of Holy Matrimony. St. Paul teaches us: "Do you not know that your body is a temple of the Holy Spirit within you, which you have from God? You are not your own; you were bought with a price. So glorify God in your body" (1 Cor 6:19–20). Chastity, therefore, is the successful integration of sexuality within us that shows an inner unity between our body and soul.

In order for us to live a life of purity and chastity, we have to undergo an apprenticeship of self-mastery. We have to accept training in true freedom. True freedom is best understood as possessing a power over our passions and desires and a strong ability to order and direct them according to moral truth and our Christian discipleship. In freedom, we can live a chaste life.

Chastity teaches us a respect and reverence for ourselves and others. It shows us the path to full human maturity, which is always found in self-donation. Chastity also instructs us on prudence, temperance, modesty, and many other related virtues. Chastity gives us pure hearts so that we can appreciate good things, wholesome affection, and healthy friendships.

The Goretti Family

Maria was raised in a devoutly Christian home. She was taught to love God and her neighbor. The life of the Gorettis showed her the value of hard work, respect for authority, and kindness to those in need. Maria was taught about respect for her body. She was raised in a home filled with love that formed her in chastity and modesty.

At the age of nine, Maria was permitted to receive her first holy communion. She absorbed every word of the priest who warned the children to preserve their souls pure and innocent, and to die rather than commit a mortal sin. Maria made this counsel the rule of her life. She would give Jesus Christ everything and guard against all sin.

Maria was a person of pure heart. After her first holy communion, when she heard some of the other children making impure jokes, she was completely shocked and couldn't understand how anyone could receive Holy Communion and say such things. Our saint's purity was not prudishness or disguised fear. It was a passionate love for Jesus Christ that would not allow anything to diminish or blemish it. Maria's love knew neither difficulty nor distance. It saw the horror of sin and chose the purity and beauty of holiness every day.

Alessandro Serenelli also saw our saint's gentleness of soul. Addicted to lust, he wanted Maria for himself and made two advances on her. At first, Maria did not understand, but then comprehended what Alessandro was suggesting. She refused him both times, telling him that it was a sin. She was calling him to virtue and holiness.

Alessandro was angered by Maria's response. He waited until she was alone. On July 5, 1902, while everyone else was in the fields working, Maria was taking care of the house duties and watching her youngest sibling.

While the child slept, Alessandro approached Maria, who was trapped and by herself, and violently demanded that she acquiesce. She screamed and fought. In radical opposition to the lust of our fallen world, and with the boldness of a saint, Maria told Alessandro, "No! No! I will not! I will not! It is a sin. God forbids it. You will go to hell, Alessandro. You will go to hell if you do it."

Alessandro would not be dissuaded. In his rage, he showed her a knife and warned Maria, "Give in or die!" With a resolution for her purity of heart and a burning love for Jesus Christ, little Maria roared like a lion, "No, I will not! No! It is a sin!" Alessandro lunged at Maria and began to viciously stab her fourteen times. She fell on the floor bloody and wounded and a day later, died from the attack.

Maria's heroic death is an inspiring testimony to the utter importance of purity and chastity in our lives and in our discipleship to the Lord Jesus. In desiring to see God, we must labor—even to point of blood—to honor our bodies and those of others and seek to order our desires according to God's law and goodness.

Workshop for Holiness

In our world today, sexual expression is viewed in terms of gaining maturity, enjoyable leisure, and accomplishment. Love and responsibility as a part of our sexual expression are dismissed as restrictive, antiquated, or unrealistic. People view sexual acts as a means of release or selfish gratification. Human dignity and personal worth are not a part of this contemporary game.

Our fallen world has forgotten the importance of chastity and self-donation in the maturation of a young person. Some people falsely believe that a loose expression of our sexual powers somehow bestow maturity or wisdom. In reality, such a loose moral life only causes broken hearts, confusion, egotism, and a growing sense of meaninglessness. For us to grow in maturity, we must nurture a life of chastity and give ourselves as a sincere gift to others in virtue, selfless service, and holy friendships. Eventually, within the sacrament of Holy Matrimony, the sexual powers become a part of this self-donation. These are the lessons of chastity. When it is lived well, we have a pure heart, and then we can see God.

As we seek a purity of heart, this chapter concludes with this Examination of Conscience:

EXAMINATION OF CONSCIENCE

- Do I treat my body and the bodies of others as temples of the Holy Spirit?

- Do I view Holy Matrimony as a sacrament given by God and the only proper place for the expression of my sexual powers?

- Have I been open to children? Do I use artificial birth control?

- Have I used in vitro fertilization technologies?

- Have I or my spouse had a sterilization procedure?

- Do I willfully entertain impure thoughts or desires?

- Do I deliberately look at impure images on the internet, television, videos, plays, pictures, or movies? Do I deliberately read impure materials?

- Have I committed any impure acts with myself (i.e., masturbation)?

- Have I committed any impure acts with another: prostitution, fornication (premarital sex), adultery (sex with a married person), or homosexual acts?

- Have I visited questionable places of "adult entertainment" known for impurity?

- Have I attended parties or other social engagements that are known to be occasions of sin?

- Do I engage in sexual foreplay reserved for marriage?

- Have I listened to jokes or music that is harmful to chastity? Have I purposely danced in a provocative manner?

- Have I made unwelcomed sexual advances towards another?

- Have I purposely dressed immodestly?

CHAPTER SEVEN

The Work for Peace in Our Relationship With God and With Others

*"Blessed are the peacemakers, for they
shall be called sons of God."*
Matthew 5:9

Peace in Our Day

We all desire peace. Oftentimes our definition of peace can be incomplete or short-sighted. Peace is not just the absence of violence or tension but the tranquility of order. This tranquility is present when all the right people are doing all the right things. Peace, therefore, is a gift from God and the workings of His grace, since only grace can heal our fallenness and give us a right relationship with God and our neighbor. In our waywardness, we need God's help. Peace only comes from above.

In order for God to bless us with peace, we need a constant conversion to Jesus Christ. Conversion always points us towards greater intimacy with God in this life and in eternity. Peace is not, therefore, a human work but the movement of God through a person with a contrite heart. The person seeking conversion is drawn and moved by grace to respond to the work of God in, with, and through Him. He must trust God's Providence and allow grace to change him. In this way, tranquility is given and peace comes forth.

In order for conversion to bring about peace, we have to continually cooperate with grace. Deeper conversion to Jesus Christ should lead to a radical reorientation of our whole lives. It causes a new set of priorities and a redefinition of things like faith, mercy, hope, freedom, love, chastity, and kindness. Conversion is an on-going process of turning away from evil. It summons us to a stronger desire and resolution to change our lives every day according to God's will and goodness.

Conversion can sometimes cause pain and sadness. We are leaving one way of life and beginning another. There can be an affliction in our spirit and repentance in our hearts as we realize, on one hand, the wickedness of sin and the darkness of where we have been, while on the other hand, the beauty of holiness and the greatness to which we are called. This is conversion, and as we continue along its path, God is able to deepen a bond of peace between He and us, as well as between our neighbors and ourselves.

The Goretti Family

Alessandro Serenelli wanted peace. He didn't know where or how to find it. The chronology of his life is a narrative of negligence, indifference, and abuse. In his hurt and anger, he did not seek the graces of conversion.

When Alessandro was a young boy, his mother died in a mental health facility, and this loss left a great void in his life. One of his brothers was also mentally ill and still in the facility when Alessandro moved in with the Goretti family at Le Ferriere. Alessandro's other siblings were married and settled and taking care of their own lives. Throughout his childhood, Alessandro had to fend for himself. He was tossed here and there within his extended family, being cared for by a cousin in this place or an aunt in that place. There was no stability, and the young man's father had no interest in him. In short, there was no peace in Alessandro's early life. It was filled with uncertainty, rejection, and loneliness.

When Alessandro was twelve, he received an apprenticeship by the sea. He enjoyed the work, but assumed all the bad habits of undisciplined and unchaste sailors. Following the bad example of those around him, he swore and cursed. Peace would continue to elude him. He was pugnacious and quarrelsome. From this experience, young Alessandro took on a warped and darkened understanding of life, work, authority, chastity, and kindness.

When Alessandro was fifteen years old, Giovanni Serenelli decided to be a father to the young man, and they began to do farm work together. It was not a relationship of paternal and filial love. The two men did not get along and there was constant tension between them. Alessandro held intense contempt in his heart towards his father. When he was in his late teens, he accompanied his father to Le Ferriere for work. In this area, the two lived with the Goretti family, and Alessandro began to spiral downward even more.

In an act of violent lust and savage brutality, Alessandro propositioned Maria Goretti. When she called him to virtue, he attacked her with a knife, and the wounds of this attack took her life.

Alessandro was sentenced to thirty years in prison, and he still did not know peace. He was trapped in a cesspool of insecurity, wrath, and extreme shame. He was lost.

Maria appeared to him in prison and offered him the lilies-turned-tongues-of-fire and for the first time in his life he was shown mercy and gentleness. It was a decisive turning point in his life that made every difference. Through our little saint, Alessandro chose Jesus Christ and began to let grace work. Hope was awakened within him, and eventually consoling peace filled his soul. Yes, now in Jesus Christ, Alessandro knew peace.

The repentant murderer began to live a life of conversion and holiness. He served twenty-seven of his thirty year sentence, having been released early on account of good conduct (the fruit of his Christian discipleship). After his release from prison, he joined in the work of the Capuchin friars as a simple gardener and groundskeeper.

At the end of his life, Alessandro wrote a public testimony. In this spiritual legacy, he reflected back on his youth and the bad path that led him to ruin. He noted the harming influence of certain print, mass media, and bad examples. He feared that such dangerous things were still influencing the majority of young people in the world, who weren't worried or even thought about them. Alessandro indicated that there were generous and devoted people around him, but he always ignored them because his heart had surrendered to a violent force that seemed to push him towards a dark path in life. He continued in the letter by expressing his repentance and indicating his desire to go to heaven.

At the very end of his life, knowing the peace of Jesus Christ, Alessandro told the friars that he killed a saint, but after decades of penance and prayer, by God's tremendous mercy, he knew he would join her in heaven.

Workshop for Holiness

It seems peace is a popular topic for news cycles and political leaders. It's a topic that resonates within the human heart. We all want peace within ourselves, among our loved ones, in our society, and in our world. Peace, however, is not given by human machinations, treaties, and summit meetings. Peace is a gift offered to us by God. It is initiated and flourishes by the conversion of hearts.

Conversion is needed if we want peace. After a life of violence and internal suffering, Alessandro found peace only in Jesus Christ. This same path of peace is offered to each of us and to our world today.

The process of conversion and the path to peace are not easy. We have to allow our fallenness and inclinations to dark paths to be forgiven, corrected, and healed. We have to allow God's grace to make us better people and disciples.

To help us along our path to peace, this chapter concludes with an Examination of Conscience:

EXAMINATION OF CONSCIENCE

- Do I look to God as the source of my peace?

- Do I seek to be an instrument of peace to others?

- Have I sought to do good with self-seeking ulterior motives?

- Do I look for opportunities to show compassion to others? Am I willing to receive the compassion of others?

- Have I delighted in seeing the hurt or suffering of others?

- Have I physically or emotionally hurt another person?

- Have I been an accomplice in the hurtful or offensive actions of others?

- Have I been prejudiced or shown discrimination to others based on their race, culture, gender, or religion?

- Do I deliberately deceive others or injure others by lies?

- Do I get angry or impatient with others?

- Am I lazy in my duties and responsibilities?

- Am I jealous or envious of others?

- Am I proud, revengeful, or hateful towards others?

- Have I abused alcohol or used illegal drugs?

- Do I care for the environment and the world around me?

CHAPTER EIGHT

Our Martyr's Legacy and Our Summons to Suffer for the Sake of Righteousness

"Blessed are those who are persecuted for righteousness'
sake, for theirs is the kingdom of heaven."
Matthew 5:10

For the Sake of Righteousness

In God's plan of salvation, the Son became a human being, lived a fully human life, suffered a torturous death, and rose on the third day. Suffering is a part of the redemptive plan by which the kingdom of sin and death are destroyed and we are reconciled to God the Father. Jesus' violent death was not the result of chance or coincidence, but an essential part of the plan of salvation. By his suffering, we are healed, saved, and sanctified.

As disciples of the Lord Jesus, we are also called to suffer for the sake of righteousness. As we endure such sufferings, we allow grace to work in both transforming us and in reaching the hearts of others around us. While never easy or comfortable, the suffering of the Christian believer is a source of tremendous grace and goodness.

Little Saint Maria Goretti understood this great lesson, and she willingly suffered for the sake of righteousness.

The Goretti Family

St. Maria Goretti was confirmed when she was six years old by Bishop Giulio Boschi (who later became a Cardinal). Before her confirmation, Maria made her first confession. In both sacraments, the little girl distinguished herself by her sincerity of faith and zeal to please the Lord Jesus. She was blessed with an attentive and sensitive heart to the things of God. Shortly after her confirmation, the family moved from the west coast of Italy to the east coast for work.

At the family's new home in Le Ferriere, Maria worked hard and sought to live the virtues of a good Christian. When she was eleven, she asked her mother when she would receive her first holy communion since she couldn't live any longer without Jesus. Her mother was concerned since Maria could not read or write and the family could not afford the dress and clothes for the ceremony. Eventually, however, arrangements were made, and Maria would walk to a neighboring town every week for eleven months to receive instruction for the sacrament. She intensified her virtues and service in order to prepare her soul for Jesus Christ.

Maria couldn't read or write with a pencil, but in her preparation for the sacrament, she wrote her own beautiful story of holiness. As the day of her first holy communion approached, the town turned out in support: one family provided her with shoes, another the veil, and another a crown of flowers. Assunta allowed her daughter to wear her own earrings. Everything was set.

In receiving Jesus in the Holy Eucharist, Maria's countenance shined and her soul burned with radiating love for Jesus Christ. After the Mass, the other children went to the sacristy to thank the priest, but Maria stayed in the church in silent prayer to God. She offered her first holy communion for her late father whom she missed terribly and asked God for the grace to be a saint. From that day on, Maria would show a new gravity in her bearing and devotion. She had a greater sense of mission about her and became more ardent in her service and kindness to others.

Maria would need this gravity and all the graces that the Lord Jesus distributes through His holy sacraments. On July 5, 1902, our little saint was chosen by God to suffer for the sake of righteousness. When Alessandro propositioned her, Maria stood firm and declared, "No! No! I will not! I will not! It is a sin. God forbids it. You will go to hell, Alessandro. You will go to hell if you do it." When Maria refused, the would-be rapist attacked and brutally assaulted her. She died the next day, which was the eve of the Feast of Corpus Christi. In great pain, just like her Eucharistic Lord whom she loved and served so faithfully, she passed from this life to the next. In her holy death, Maria suffered for the sake of righteousness, and she gave us all a powerful testimony to a life lived in Jesus Christ.

Maria forgave Alessandro before receiving Viaticum, her last holy communion. She cried for her father and then died in peace. The word martyr means "witness" in Greek, and Maria gives an earth-shaking and resplendent witness to us of the beauty and power of purity and mercy.

On June 24, 1950, the Venerable Pope Pius XII canonized Maria Goretti and declared her a patron saint of youth. In the Catholic Church's extensive history, Maria shines as the youngest person ever canonized a saint. Over 500,000 people attended the canonization ceremony, which was the largest congregation of worshippers up to that point. Among the hundreds of thousands of people at the Mass were her mother, Assunta, and the repentant Alessandro Serenelli. There were so many people in total that the ceremony was held outside of St. Peter's Basilica. It was the first outdoor canonization Mass celebrated at the Vatican.

Maria left us a compelling legacy and wants to assist us in our own purity and mercy. She wants us to live as better Christians. From heaven, Maria Goretti is a strong miracle worker in terms of physical healings, overcoming addictions to drugs or pornography, restoring marriages, healing from a rape, and in a multitude of other ways. Our little saint continues her service to Jesus Christ and calls us all to a deeper love of God and our neighbor.

Workshop for Holiness

In life, many are inclined to easy or relaxing things. If we're not careful, we bring this inclination to our discipleship. Why cause problems? Why stand up and suffer for righteousness? Life is too difficult as it is, why make it harder? These and similar questions can eclipse or completely overshadow our summons to suffer for the sake of righteousness. In order for us to stand and suffer for righteousness, we have to allow grace to mature and conquer fear, vanity, and laziness.

Maria's life exemplified the radical choice we are all invited to make for Jesus Christ and His gospel. She shows us how to live as Christians, how to vanquish fear, and how to suffer for the sake of righteousness. In her tender age, she faced death and did not falter, compromise, or backslide in her discipleship in any way. This is her legacy. She is an example and an intercessor for us in our own witness and in our call to stand and suffer for righteousness. What will be our legacy?

As we look for the fortitude to suffer for righteousness, the chapter concludes with this Examination of Conscience:

EXAMINATION OF CONSCIENCE

- Do I look to God for the strength to live my life well?

- Do I regularly receive the sacraments and rely on God's grace?

- Am I afraid of dying or being mistreated?

- Am I willing to suffer for what is right, good, and true?

- Do I study the truths of faith and share them with others?

- Am I ashamed of my faith and virtue? Or the faith and virtue of others?

- Do I guard and protect the virtue and holiness of those entrusted to my care?

- Do I vote and participate in the public arena?

- Have I called evil things evil?

- Am I vain and afraid of what people will think of me?

- Do I remain silent in the face of evil because I'm afraid of being called names or suffering other consequences?

- Do I defend the Church and moral goodness in the public arena?

- Do I support immoral businesses or institutions?

- Do I voice opposition or boycott morally offensive aspects of our culture?

- Have I failed to stand up or walk away when irreligious, impure, or other immoral jokes or stories were being told?

An Apprenticeship in Chastity

"Chastity includes an *apprenticeship in self-mastery* which is a training in human freedom." *Catechism of the Catholic Church,* no. 2342

"All the baptized are called to chastity . . . All Christ's faithful are called to live a chaste life in keeping with their particular states of life." *Catechism of the Catholic Church,* no. 2348

General Counsel

Before entering (or re-entering) an apprenticeship of chastity, it's important for us to remember what chastity is and why we should want to be chaste. The desire to be chaste is not simply to avoid guilt or bad consequences in this life. Chastity is about living fully as a human person and as a Christian believer.

It's worth noting that chastity is expressed differently in the various vocations of the Church. Celibate chastity is the life of those called to the priesthood or consecrated service, as well as those who are single for the Lord. Celibacy is not the chastity of the married life. Marital chastity is enriched by sexual expression, and is marked by temperance and a love for one's spouse.

What is chastity then? How are we called to be chaste?

Chastity is about integrity. It's having control and harmony over our sexual desires and powers as a human person. It means we won't allow ourselves to live as an animal by instinct or as a puzzle broken among several pieces. Chastity gives us the strength to be our true selves rather than the fragmented version that lust leaves in its wake. Chastity gives us freedom and prevents us from becoming slaves to our sexual passions, following them where they lead us and doing whatever they tell us.

Chastity makes us honest. It won't tolerate double talk or duplicity. It's opposed to any behavior that is not ordered to truth and that would cause harm or impair our holistic well being.

The virtue of chastity is a personal task. It takes a particular form according to our state in life, our personality and temperament, our emotional state, the situations of our life, and an array of other considerations. Chastity is a long and exacting work. And as we cooperate with God's grace and let chastity work, it molds and shapes us so that we can truly give ourselves to others. It's a school on the gift of self.

Chastity flourishes in healthy and virtuous friendships. It gives relationships a liberty from wayward passions and orders affection and physical expression according to love and self-donation.

So, with this understanding of chastity, how can we be chaste? What are some practical steps we can take to live chastity as a good person and as a Christian believer?

Fundamental Steps

Here are some fundamental steps we can all take to live a life of faithful chastity:

- **Self-knowledge.** Each of us has to know ourselves. What do I want from other people? What do I want to give? How do I give aspects of my life to other people? What is my personality type? What is my temperament? What animates or arouses me? What emotional hurts do I carry? How do I seek consolation? What personality types am I attracted to? How do I express affection? What's the level of my sex drive? How do I handle loneliness or perceived rejection? What is my understanding of chastity? What influence in my life am I willing to give to my faith or virtue? Do I pray?

- **Ascetical practices.** Each of us has to acknowledge our fallenness and weakness and allow grace to heal and order us according to truth and goodness. Ascetical practices are small ways of saying "no" to things so that our will is strengthened, and we can say "yes" to greater things. Some options for ascetical practices include abstaining from foods, video games and the internet, fasting on Fridays or in times of temptation or distraction, simplifying our schedules, giving away material possessions we don't need, selflessly serving others, focusing on others in conversations, waking up earlier than needed, waking up quickly and not using a "snooze" button, seeking occasions for fellowship with people we don't like, avoiding procrastination and completing all tasks quickly, volunteering for the hardest or most undesirable tasks in my state in life, willingly follow the counsel of others without opinion or complaint, and so many other practices. In small ways, each of us can live an ascetical life and form our wills for a generous living out of chastity.

- **Obedience to God's commandments.** In order to truly grow as a person and let chastity become an integrated part of our lives, we have to obey God's commandments. We have to honor His majesty, the holiness of His Name,

and the sanctity of His Sabbath. On
the Sabbath, we have to join the whole
Church in worshipping God at Mass,
and we have to let our minds and
bodies rest by avoiding needless work,
as well as spending time with family
and loved ones. We have to honor our
parents since they gave us life and are
a part of us. With our neighbors, we
have to avoid harsh attitudes, violence,
impure acts, stealing, cheating, lies,
gossip, envy, and jealousy. By form-
ing our minds and hearts on the law
of God, we can discern right from
wrong in our lives and know what we
are called to do and how we are summoned to live and love.

- **Exercise of Moral Virtues.** There
  are four moral virtues. Chastity is an
  expression of temperance. The other
  three virtues are prudence, justice,
  and fortitude. Temperance is a rightly
  ordered use of good things. It assures
  our will's mastery over our instincts
  and keeps our desires and use of
  things within the limits of goodness.
  Some acts of temperance via chastity
  could include clear boundaries for
  affection and dating relationships,

moderate use of alcohol, avoiding idle time alone, limited private use of the internet, public location of computers, tempered use of television viewing, regular sleep habits, healthy eating, an exercise plan or sports involvement, appropriate levels of self-disclosure in conversations, a custody of the eyes and senses in moments of temptation or distraction, avoiding flirting or any form of flattery, and several other ways. Living temperance in chastity is a life's work. We are called to cooperate with grace and do our best.

• **Fidelity to Prayer.** Everything flows from and leads to the Holy Mass. If we are not participating in Sunday Mass, then we are trying to drive a car without gas. We must attend Sunday Mass. In the true worship of God, He generously pours out His grace upon us. This is the grace we need to live a life of virtue and chastity. Without God's grace, we can do nothing. Some other acts of prayer we can consider are daily Mass, regular reception of Confession, reading the Bible, personal meditation time, adoration of the Blessed Sacrament, the Liturgy

of the Hours, the Rosary, the Divine
Mercy Chaplet, the reading of spiritual books, and many other prayerful
practices of the Church. Each of these
practices can help us to live a chaste
life through the grace of God.

These are some of the practical ways that each of us
can be apprenticed in chastity, which is a free and life-
giving way of life shown to us by the Lord Jesus and
offered to us every day.

St. Maria Goretti exemplified this virtue by her blood.
In her life and death, she showed us the supreme value
and importance of this liberating virtue. She dwells now
in heaven constantly interceding for us and offering us
encouragement on our own journey to live a life of chastity. St. Maria Goretti, pray for us!

APPENDIX TWO

An Apprenticeship in Mercy

"It is not in our power not to feel or to forget an offense; but the heart that offers itself to the Holy Spirit turns injury into compassion and purifies the memory in transforming the hurt into intercession." *Catechism of the Catholic Church,* no. 2843

"Forgiveness also bears witness that, in our world, love is stronger than sin." *Catechism of the Catholic Church,* no. 2844

General Counsel

For Christian believers, mercy is at the center of everything we do. Our faith illustrates for us that we are undeserving recipients of the mercy of God, and this core truth influences everything we do. It especially affects the way we give mercy and offer forgiveness. And so, as Christian disciples, we do not have the option of willfully refusing mercy. How, then, do we offer mercy?

Mercy requires that we allow our intellect and will to order and align our emotions to what is true, good, and beautiful. A raw expression of emotion, so popular in our society, will not allow grace to work. We must mature and quiet our emotions, allowing them to be expressed in positive and edifying ways. In what ways can we let our intellect and will act? What process can we follow to allow grace and virtue to work? How can I become a person of mercy?

Fundamental Steps

Here are five steps that can assist us in cooperating with grace and growing as a person of mercy:

- **Receive mercy.** In order to give something, we have to first possess it (cf. Acts 3:6). In our own lives and discipleship, we have to receive mercy from God and others. First and foremost, this means frequenting the Sacrament of Confession. It also means allowing God's grace to be known and felt in our lives. Additionally, we have to accept the mercy of others. Oftentimes, either out of scrupulosity or shame, we will avoid the mercy that others offer for our mistakes or offenses. We have to humble ourselves and receive the mercy that is offered to us. This is our first step.

- **Pray.** When we neglect a life of prayer, we end up trying to figure things out on our own. Inevitably, in our

fallenness, we can be persuaded by all
sorts of bad spirits. We have to turn to
prayer and allow for the transforma-
tion of our hearts and minds so that
we may know what is good, pleasing,
and perfect to God (cf. Rom 12:1–2).
In prayer, we encounter the God of
mercy and He teaches and forms us.
He gives us the strength and the perse-
verance to forgive. If we hit a wall with
mercy due to an offense to ourselves
or a loved one, we must turn to prayer
and ask for a tender and forgiving
heart. This is our second step.

- **Name the offense.** Oftentimes when
something difficult or insulting has
happened, we try to forget it and move
along. Such a reaction, however, does
not help us to show mercy. In our
process to forgive, we have to name
the offense. Like Jesus in the graveyard
of Genesseret who ordered the fallen
spirit to name himself, so we must
name our offense (see Lk 8:30). In
naming the offense, it looses its power
over us (cf. Jn 3:14–15). This is our
third step.

- **Speak Words of Mercy.** At this point
in our process, we turn to the Lord

Jesus and cling to him. We name the person who has given the offense, and we verbally say that we forgive this person, and we ask God to bless them (cf. Lk 7:48). This is not legitimizing any offense or diminishing any pain. This is the act of a Christian believer, who knows mercy and in his love for God, desires to give mercy to another. It is absolving the debt and what is due to us in acknowledging a greater order of loving kindness. This is an act of the intellect and will, not of the emotions. This is our fourth step.

- **Order our Emotions.** After giving mercy to our offender, we must name and expel any bad emotions that may arise: pain, bitterness, pride, anger, or any other negative force. We must name these dark influences and remove them. If we are struggling with particular emotions, we should fall on God's grace and repeat our fourth step. In this process, much suffering might be endured as God heals our soul through our love and mercy (cf. Mt 8:8). This is the path to forgiveness and freedom.

This is a practical process by which we can slowly move to an act of mercy. It will not be an easy process. Depending on the offense, it might be one of the hardest things we'll ever do in life and in our discipleship.

As she lay dying, St. Maria Goretti showed her assailant great mercy and even hoped that he might one day join her in heaven. Our virgin-martyr shows us Jesus, manifests His mercy, and leads us along His way by her example and intercession. St. Maria Goretti, pray for us!

A Prayer to St. Maria Goretti for Purity and Holiness

O St. Maria Goretti, strengthened by God's grace, thou didst not hesitate, even at the age of twelve, to sacrifice life itself to defend thy virginal purity. Look graciously on the unhappy human race that has strayed far from the path of eternal salvation. Teach us that promptness in fleeing temptation that will help us avoid anything that could offend Jesus. Obtain for me a great horror of impurity and of all sin, so that I may live a holy life on earth and win eternal glory in heaven. Amen.

Our Father, Hail Mary, Glory Be . . .

Bibliography

Catechism of the Catholic Church. Libreria Editrice Vaticana: Vatican City, 1997.

Church Teachings:

The works listed here are provided as useful references for those who would like more information about the major topics covered in this book.

Pope St. John XXIII. *Pacem in Terris.* Libreria Editrice Vaticana: Vatican City, 1963. http://w2.vatican.va/content/john-xxiii/en/encyclicals/documents/hf_j-xxiii_enc_11041963_pacem.html.

Pope St. John Paul II. *Dives in Misericordia.* Libreria Editrice Vaticana: Vatican City, 1980. http://w2.vatican.va/content/john-paul-ii/en/encyclicals/documents/hf_jp-ii_enc_30111980_dives-in-misericordia.html.

———. *Evangelium Vitae.* Libreria Editrice Vaticana: Vatican City, 1995. http://w2.vatican.va/content/john-paul-ii/en/encyclicals/documents/hf_jp-ii_enc_25031995_evangelium-vitae.html.

———. *Familiaris Consortio.* Libreria Editrice Vaticana: Vatican City, 1981. http://w2.vatican.va/content/john -paul-ii/en/apost_exhortations/documents/hf_jp-ii _exh_19811122_familiaris-consortio.html.

———. *Laborem Exercens.* Libreria Editrice Vaticana: Vatican City, 1981. http://w2.vatican.va/content/ john-paul-ii/en/encyclicals/documents/hf_jp-ii_enc _14091981_laborem-exercens.html.

———. *Redemptoris Custos.* Libreria Editrice Vaticana: Vatican City, 1989. http://w2.vatican.va/content/john -paul-ii/en/apost_exhortations/documents/hf_jp-ii _exh_15081989_redemptoris-custos.html.

———. *Salvifici Doloris.* Libreria Editrice Vaticana: Vatican City, 1984. http://w2.vatican.va/content/john -paul-ii/en/apost_letters/1984/documents/hf_jp-ii _apl_11021984_salvifici-doloris.html.

Books for further reading:

Cantalamessa, Raniero. *Poverty.* New York: Alba House, 1997.

———. *Virginity.* New York: Alba House, 1995.

Eden, Dawn. *The Thrill of the Chaste: Catholic Edition.* Notre Dame: Ave Maria Press, 2015.

Groeschel, Benedict. *The Courage to be Chaste.* New York: Paulist Press, 1988.

Kirby, Jeffrey. *Lord, Teach Us to Pray.* Charlotte: Saint
Benedict Press, 2014.

West, Christopher. *Theology of the Body for Beginners.*
Milwaukee: Ascension Press, 2009.

CPSIA information can be obtained at www.ICGtesting.com
Printed in the USA
LVOW08s2243071016
507222LV00001B/63/P